A BUG TRAVELS FAR

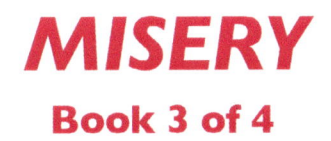

MISERY
Book 3 of 4

DOREN CUMMINGS
ILLUSTRATED BY HUGOSHI

A Bug Travels Far
Misery
©2025, Doren Cummings

All rights reserved. This book or any portion thereof may not be reproduced or used in any manner whatsoever without the express written permission of the publisher except for the use of brief quotations in a book review.

ISBN: 979-8-35094-163-0

Dedicated to the authors of banned books.

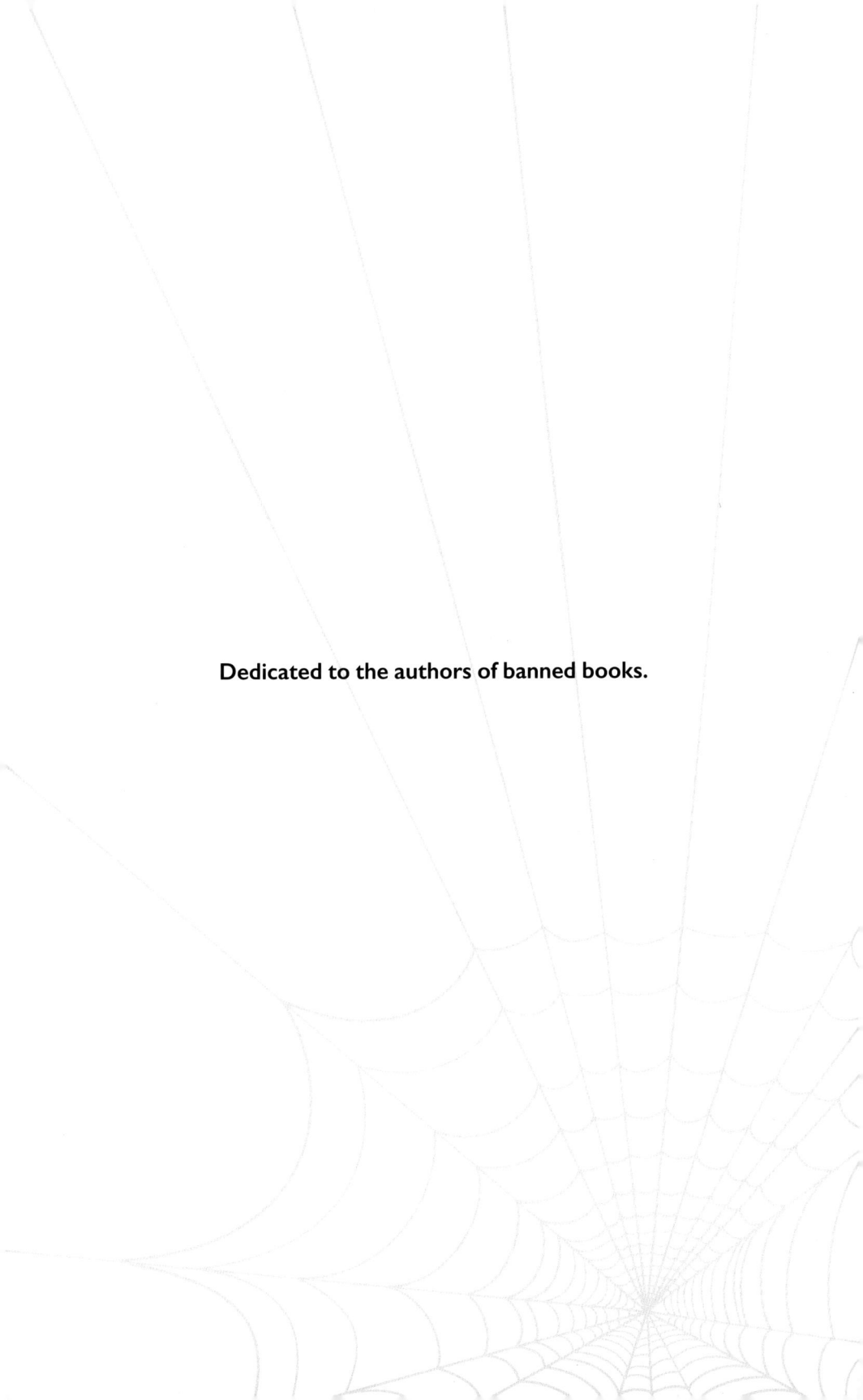

Ty Fly wandered through the airport, searching for his flight home to Boston.

"The big flyball game is today," he said, glancing at the clock. "I can't be late."

The past two days had been a whirlwind. After getting trapped in a car, Ty ended up in New York City, where he reunited with his brother, Tom, who had recently moved there. Tom struggled to accept that Ty was a transbug—born a girl but always knowing he was a boy. During their time together, Tom began to understand and support Ty for who he truly was.

Now, with Tom's support, Ty was determined to face his team back in Boston. They had bullied him for being "different," but he was ready to show them that being true to yourself was something to be proud of.

Time	Destination	Gate	Flight
09:00	Boston	A3	143
09:00	Paris	B1	2472
10:00	Miami	C3	6674
10:30	Turks and Caicos	D2	4763

08:50

Ty stopped at the flight information screen.

"The next flight to Boston leaves in ten minutes?" he gasped.

He maneuvered through the bustling crowd, scanning for his gate. The flyball game could not start without him.

Suddenly, the person in front of him came to an abrupt halt.

SMACK

Ty crashed to the ground, momentarily dazed.

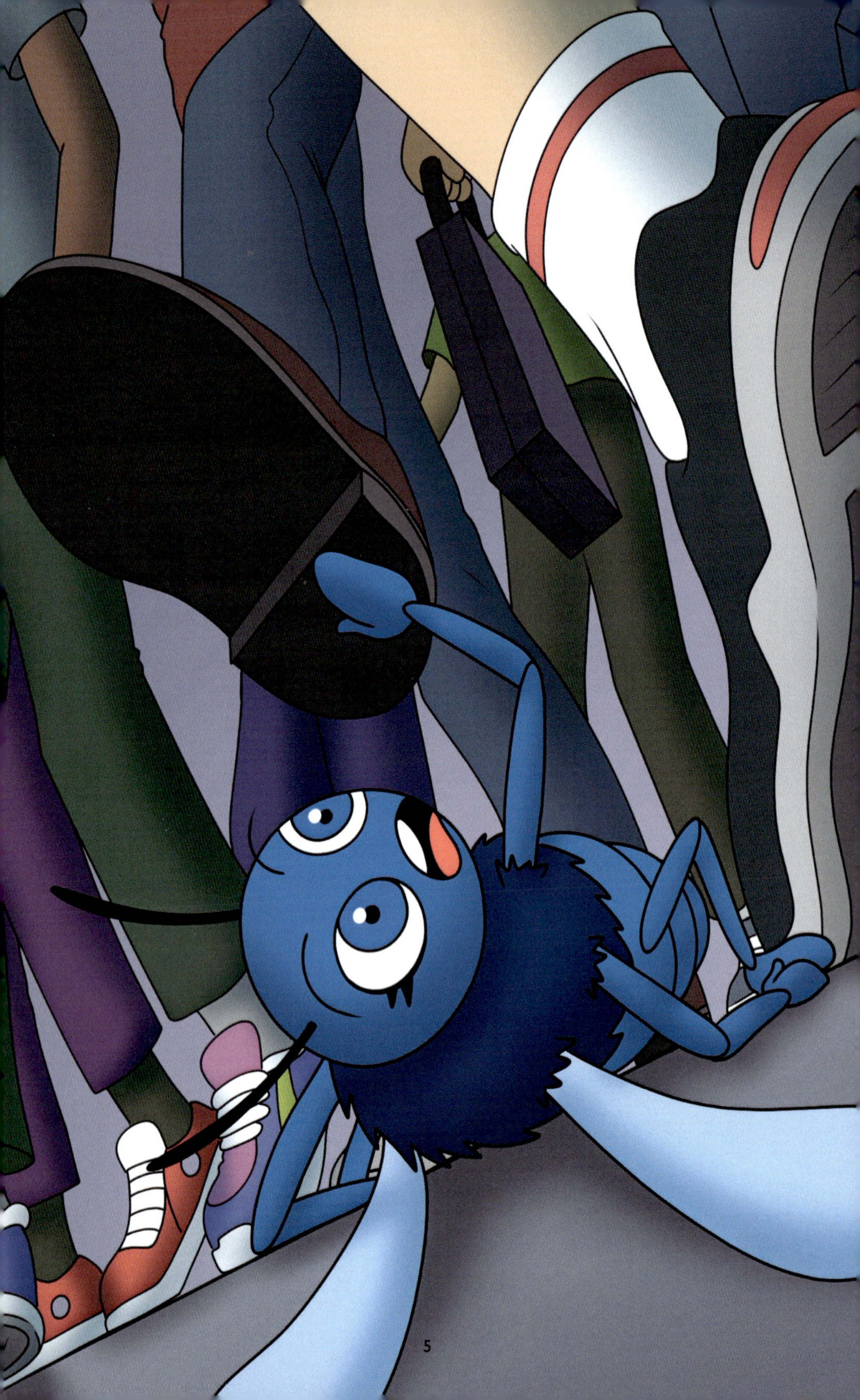

He shook his head, then flapped his wings furiously—just in time to dodge a heavy footstep.

"Another close call," he muttered, zooming back into the air.

Up ahead, he spotted the boarding gate.

Ty cruised through the long tunnel at lightning speed, a blur against the bright windows.

This is the fastest I've ever flown, he thought.

He darted through the airplane door just as it was closing.

"Shoo!" the flight attendant said, frowning. "These bugs think they can catch a ride wherever they want."

"I made it!" Ty exclaimed, beaming with pride. "I'm one step closer to home."

Ty flew over to the cockpit and landed on the control panel, eyes wide.

"Wow," he breathed, gazing at the maze of buttons and switches. "Tom is never going to believe this!"

"Dang flies!" the co-pilot snapped, giving Ty a dirty look and swatting at him.

Ty made his way to the back of the plane to find an empty seat. "It's smooth sailing from here," he said confidently.

He looked over at the window and noticed a spider. *Who knew bugs did all this traveling?* he pondered.

All the bugs he had met so far had been friendly. "Hi," he greeted warmly. "I'm Ty Fly."

The spider stared blankly at Ty, a cold stillness in its stare. Ty noticed one of its legs twitching, not out of nervousness but perhaps readiness? The overhead lights flickered.

"I'm not a fan of flying," Ty confessed, trying to make small talk. "Kind of ironic, isn't it? A fly who doesn't enjoy flying." He laughed softly.

The spider crept closer, their eyes narrowing as they inspected Ty.

"Are you a boy or a girl?" they asked bluntly, their tone sharp.

Ty had heard this question before. "I'm a boy," he answered, keeping his voice steady.

"Really?" the spider scoffed, looking him up and down with a smirk. "You don't look like any boy I've ever seen. Are you sure you're not just mixed up, or perhaps trying to trick me?" they added, their voice cold and accusatory.

"I'm Annie, and it's obvious I'm all girl," she declared, arrogantly.

FREE

An awkward silence followed. Ty noticed the bathroom and changed the subject.

"Ah, first class at its finest," he joked. "Nothing like a smelly bathroom to make a fly feel right at home."

He excused himself, grateful for a moment to collect his thoughts.

"Breathe in…breathe out," Ty chanted, meditating.

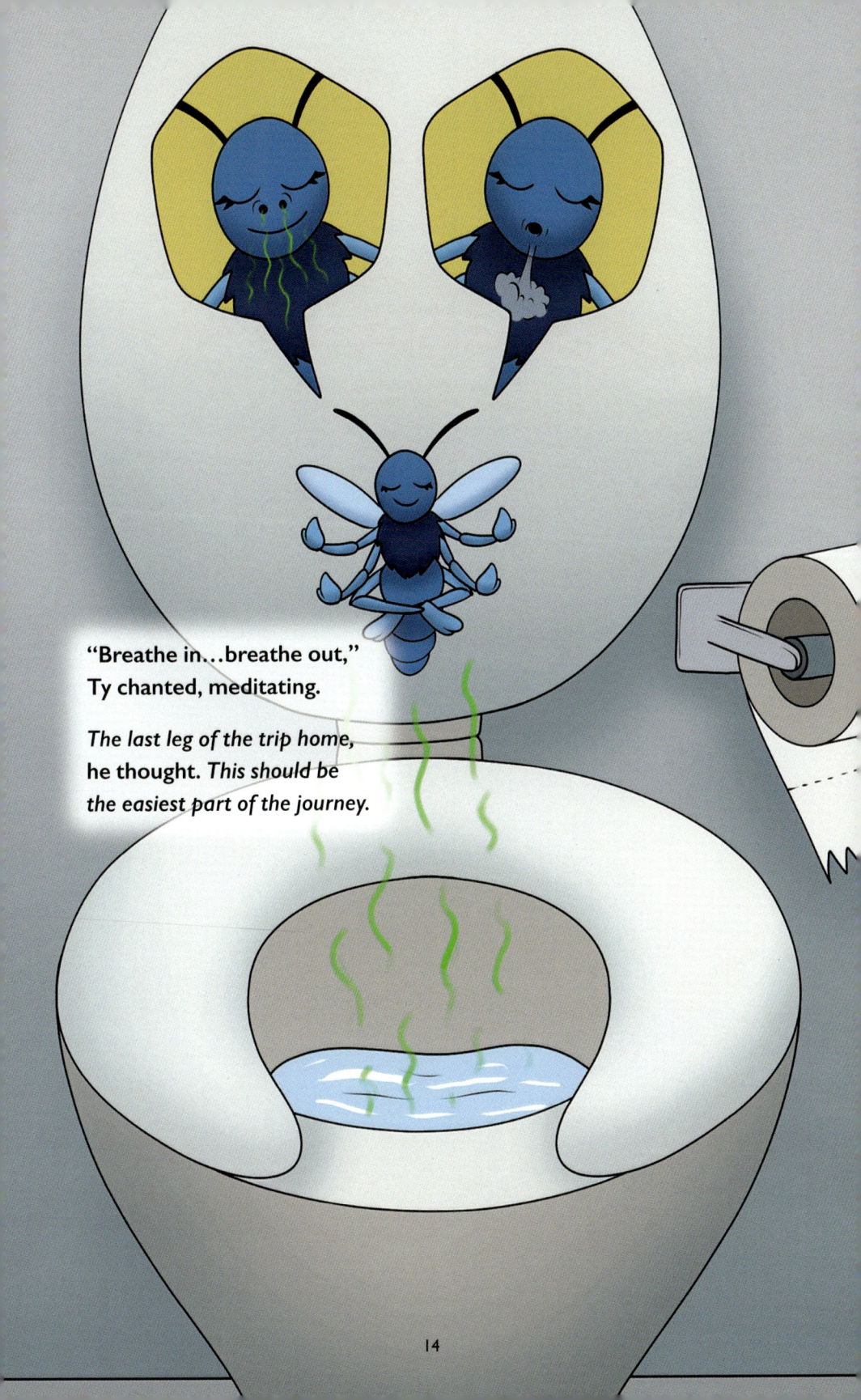

The last leg of the trip home, he thought. *This should be the easiest part of the journey.*

When the door opened, Ty zipped out and saw the flight attendant prepping the snack cart. He glanced at the options, hoping for some breakfast.

"Eww, get out of here," the flight attendant said, wrinkling her nose. "Gross fly!"

Ty went back to his seat. He stared out the window, spooked by the storm.

Suddenly, Annie was right behind him, leaning in close.

"The rain," she whispered, "sometimes it gives me the blues."

Ty saw her reflection in the window, her eyes fixed with a disturbing smile. A shiver ran down his back as he felt something unsettling about her.

"Umm, I'm really tired, Annie," Ty said, trying to be polite. "I didn't sleep well last night. I have to get to Boston for a big game at the flyball park today. I'm going to take a nap and rest up."

"Sure," Annie chittered, her voice oddly cheerful.

"You must be feeling oogie."

"This is Captain Bessie Coleman speaking. Welcome to flight 143, New York to Boston," she announced.

"We are happy to have you on board this morning. The weather looks a little rocky, but just sit back and relax. It's a short trip up the East Coast. We'll get you there in one piece, I promise."

As the plane gently rumbled, Ty closed his eyes, trying to push away the discomfort from Annie's earlier comments. The hum of the engines and the soft flicker of the dimmed lights lulled him into a deep, uneasy sleep.

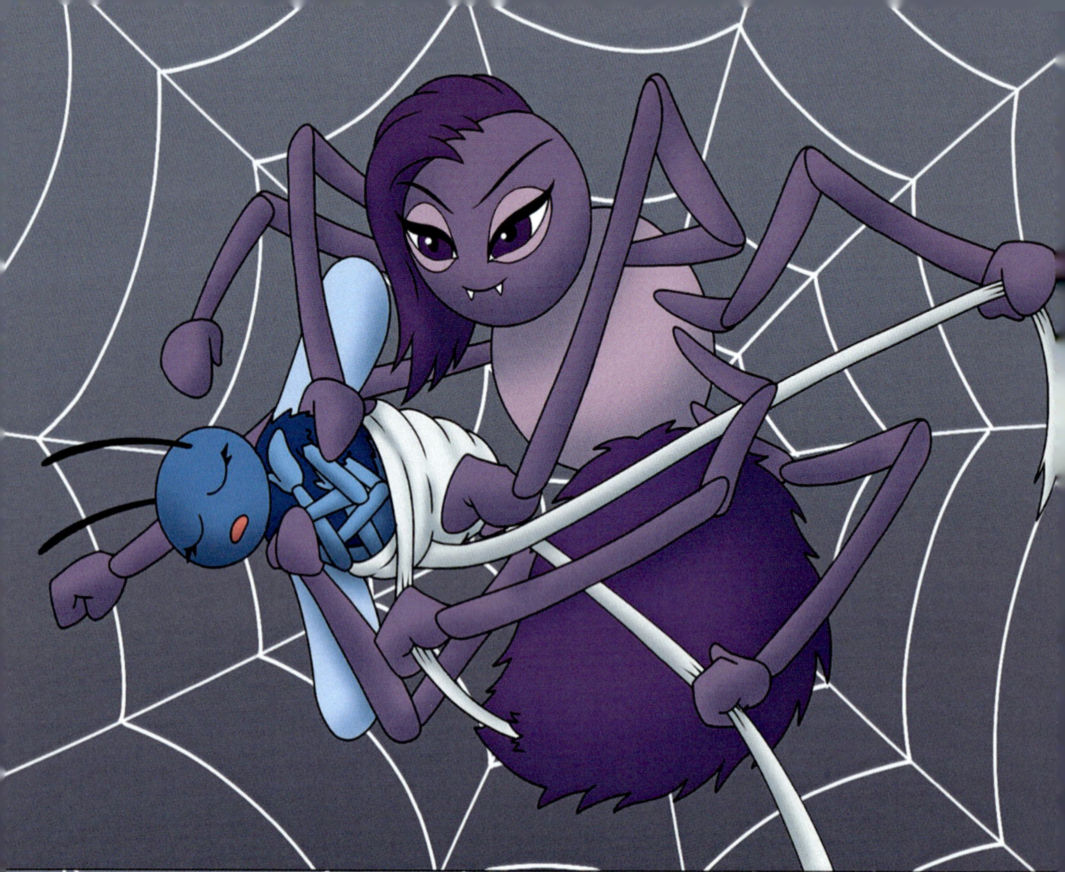

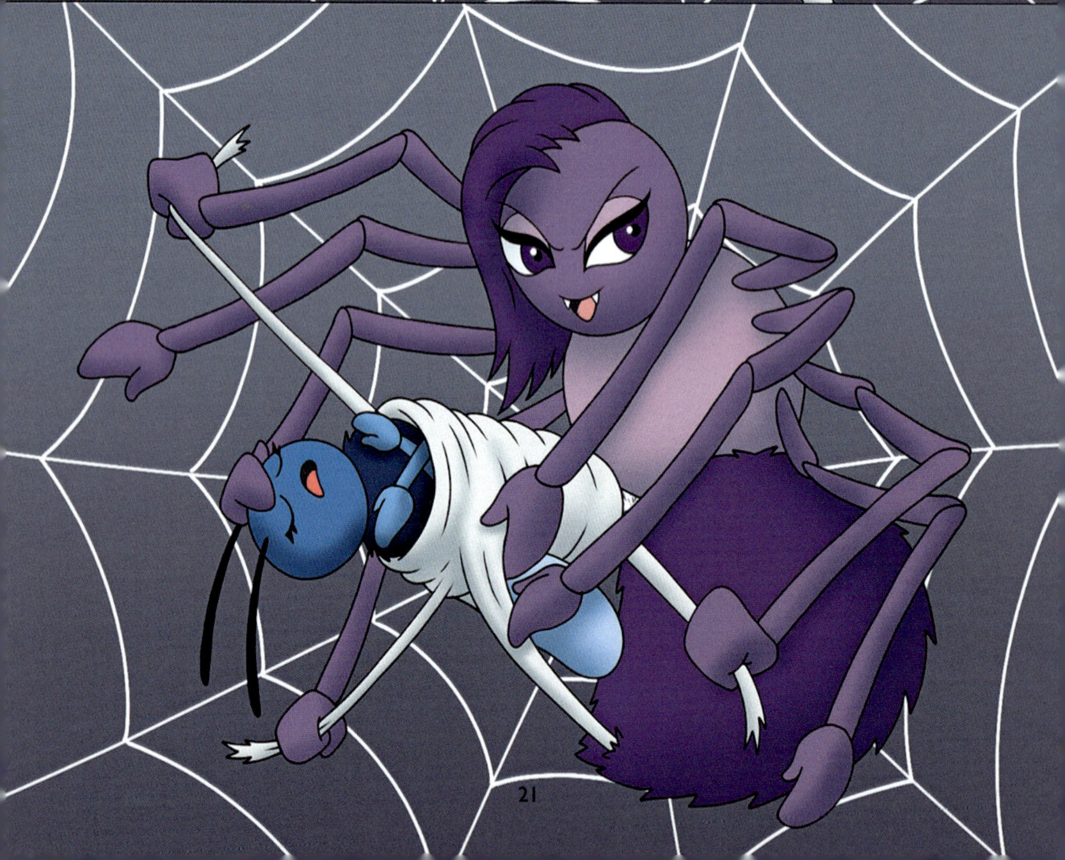

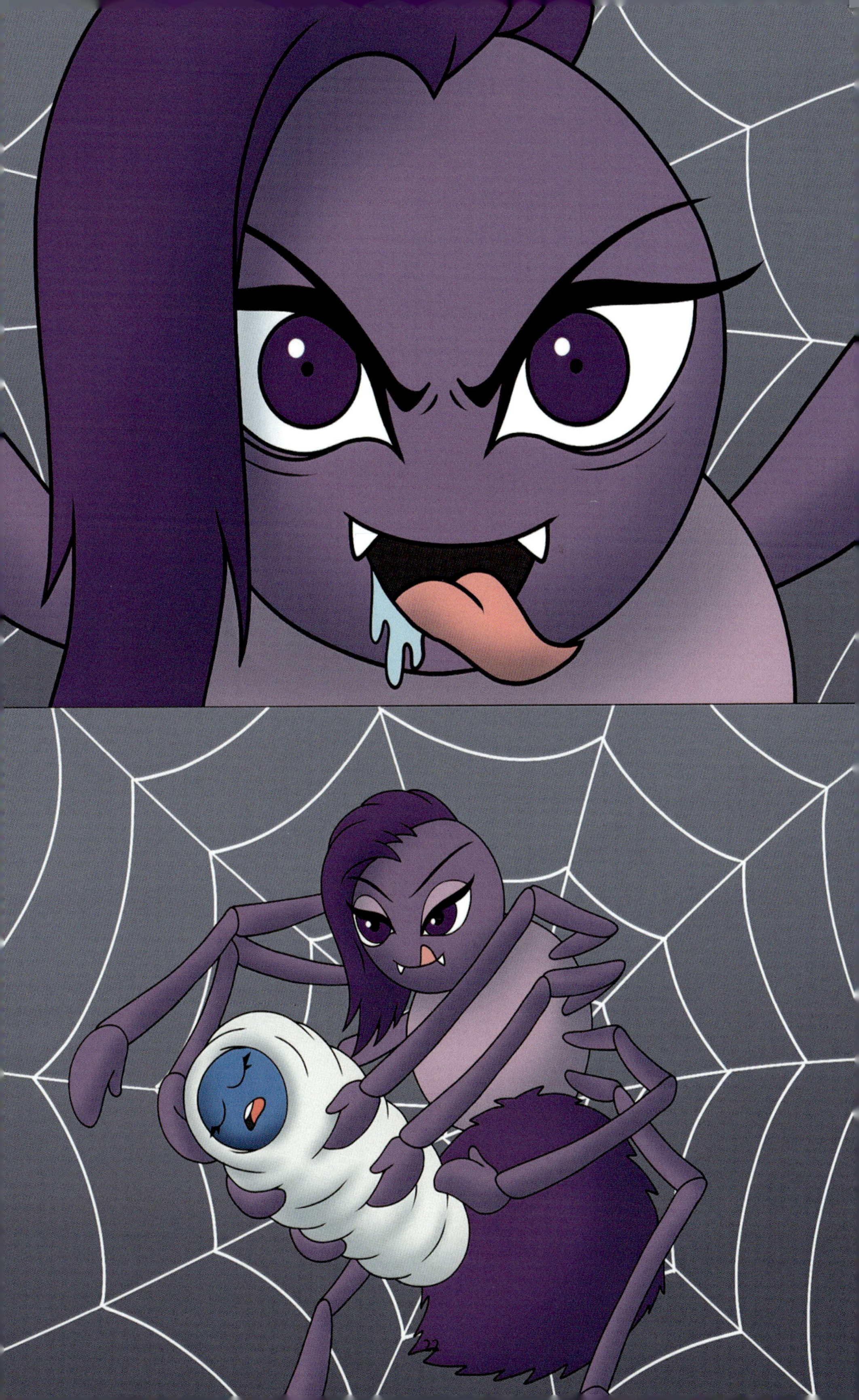

23

Ty had vivid dreams. He imagined himself at practice with his team, chatting with Kelsey Tick and hearing Will Grasshopper sing. He felt the breeze from the newspaper swatting at Honey Bee and the tight hugs from his family. It felt like he was safely wrapped in his blanket at home, comfortable and secure.

"Mmmm," Ty groaned, struggling to move his wings.

They were stuck. His eyes fluttered open, slowly taking in his surroundings. Annie's eight legs formed a cage around him, like the bars of a cold, dark jail. Ty found his wings and legs caught in her silky web, trapping him like a prisoner.

"Annie! What are you doing?" Ty cried out, struggling against the web.

"Should I break your wings one at a time?" Annie snarled, a wicked in her eyes as she raised a leg, threateningly.

"Annie, I thought we were friends," Ty pleaded, his voice desperate. "It's the humans who are our enemies, not each other. We need to stick together," he added, hoping to sway her.

Annie laughed. "Spiders and flies are not friends, Ty. It's basic science. Haven't you heard of the food chain or survival of the fittest?"

Ty's heart sank as he realized the truth—he was Annie's prey. This was the most danger he had faced on his entire adventure.

Ty felt exposed, like he was on display, as he noticed the people in line for the bathroom staring at him trapped in Annie's web.

"Dad, a black widow just caught that housefly," the teen said, his eyes wide with excitement. "Nature's wonder is happening right in front of us."

He quickly pulled out his phone and started recording.

"What a death trap! This is going to make great content," he said, grinning.

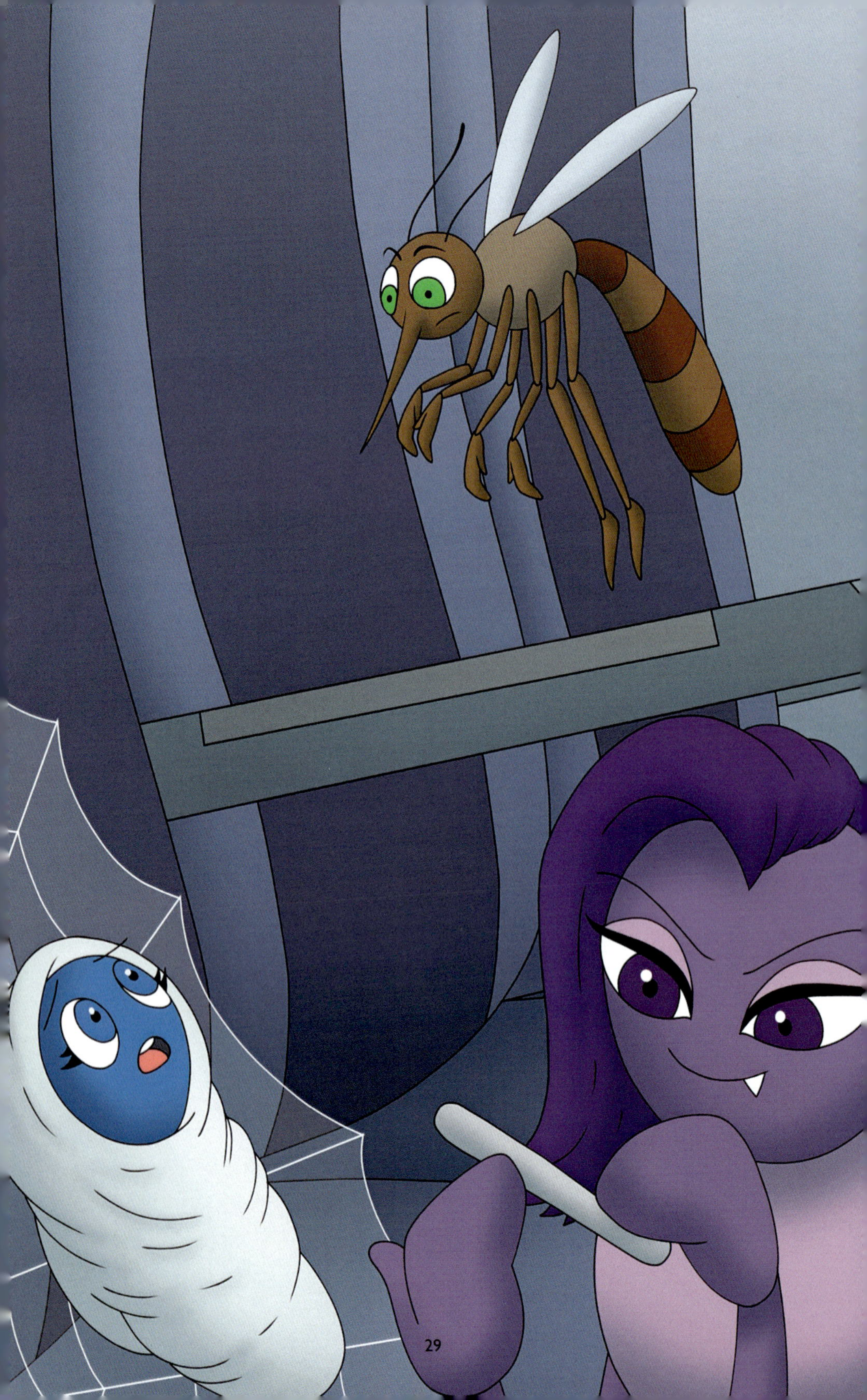

Ty wiggled and twisted, desperately trying to break free from Annie's web. When he fluttered his wings, they made a harsh humming sound.

"You're not going anywhere, Ty," Annie sneered. "I'm bringing you to the family barbecue. I can't show up empty-handed."

Realizing there was no reasoning with Annie, Ty frantically looked around for help. He spotted a mosquito lazily buzzing by.

"Hey, over here!" he called out, his voice filled with quiet desperation.

The mosquito glanced at Ty, then at Annie. It hovered for a moment, clearly intrigued by the situation.

"Can you cut one of these threads loose?" Ty begged.

The mosquito laughed. "You want me to risk my wings for you? Please. I've got more important things to do. Besides, watching this is way more entertaining. Better you than me, fly."

With a dismissive buzz, the mosquito flew away, leaving Ty feeling even more trapped.

Ty watched as the mosquito flew over to a passenger and landed. The pest pulled its head back and jabbed the human's bare arm. Ty couldn't help but gawk as the mosquito's body swelled with blood.

WHACK!

The passenger's hand came down hard on the mosquito—a direct hit. Without a second thought, they flicked the dead bug onto the floor.

"This is misery," Ty gulped, feeling his hope of escape fading.

The captain's voice crackled over the loudspeaker. "We are preparing for landing, folks," she said. "There's some turbulence due to the cloudy day here in Boston. We'll try to make it as smooth as possible."

The plane shifted and rocked. Ty noticed some of the passengers looking nervous. The constant motion only deepened the growing sense of dread in the pit of his stomach.

32

The thunderstrikes rumbled outside, and a sudden gust of wind rocked the plane. Ty felt the web around him tear, and a few strands began to loosen. It dawned on him that Annie had spun the web in haste during his short nap—it wasn't as secure as she'd thought.

Ty wiggled his wings and legs, slowly working them loose through the gaps in the web. With each jolt of the plane's landing, he managed to free himself a bit more. Annie was being tossed around by the plane's rough descent, her focus no longer on him.

"Welcome to the Commonwealth. Boston's local time is 10:30 a.m., and it looks like the sun is trying to come out. It's been a pleasure flying with you all today," Captain Coleman announced.

As the passengers began gathering their bags and filing out of the plane, Ty knew he had to act quickly.

The flight attendants began to check each seat as the plane emptied.

Maybe a human will help me this time, Ty thought desperately.

He beat his wings together as hard as he could, trying to get their attention.

"HммEzzLaaP," Ty yelled, his voice strained with effort.

"Quiet, fly," Annie snapped, her eyes narrowing as she tried to regain control.

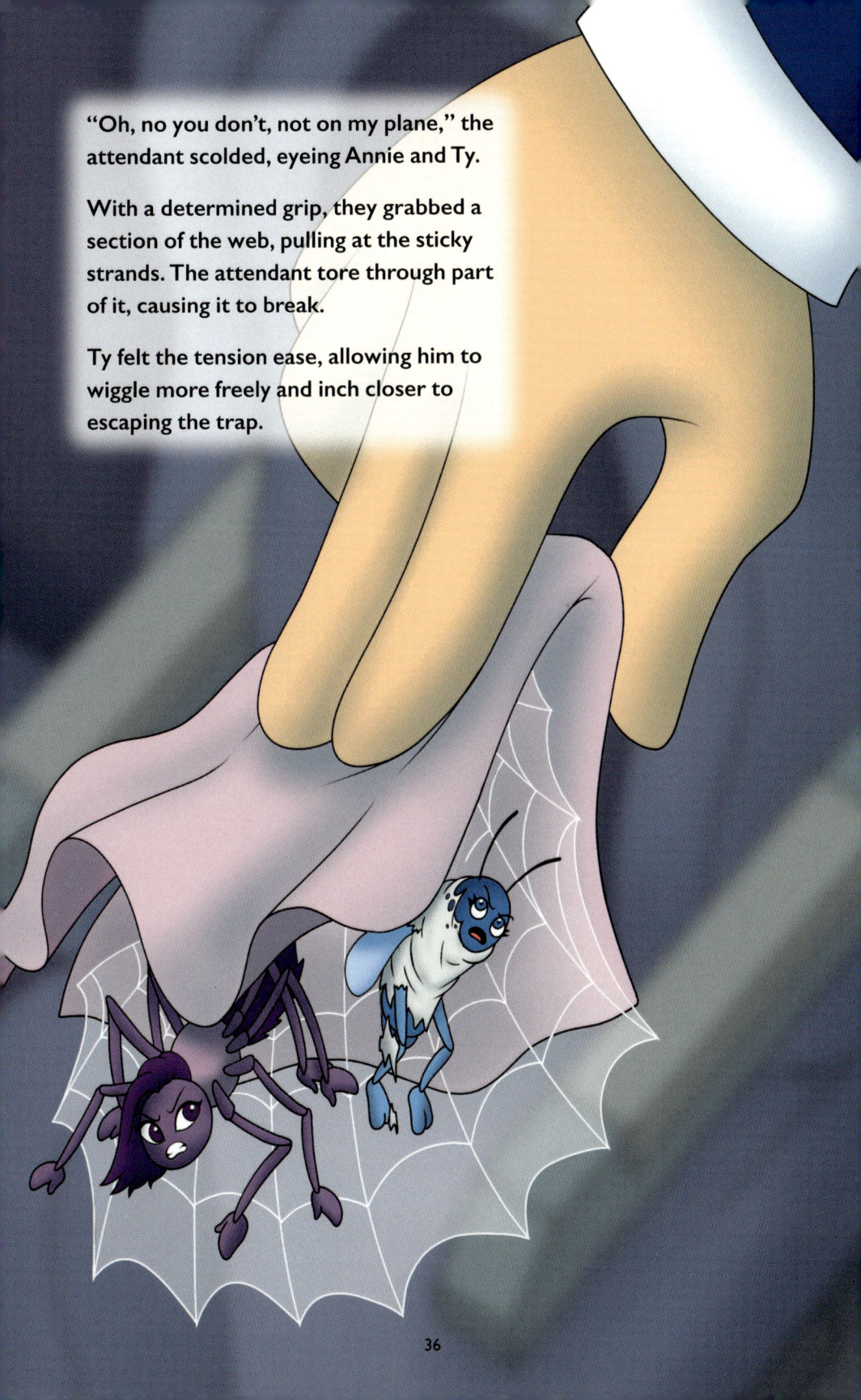

"Oh, no you don't, not on my plane," the attendant scolded, eyeing Annie and Ty.

With a determined grip, they grabbed a section of the web, pulling at the sticky strands. The attendant tore through part of it, causing it to break.

Ty felt the tension ease, allowing him to wiggle more freely and inch closer to escaping the trap.

37

"These bugs are disgusting," the attendant grumbled, shaking their head in annoyance.

Ty and Annie both dangled from the torn web, fighting for leverage.

"You won't escape me!" Annie hissed, her grip tightening as she tried to hold on.

"Save yourself! Why are you still trying to capture me?" Ty shot back, pushing her away as he fought for his freedom.

Annie and Ty's wrestling loosened the last strands of the web holding Ty's wings. With one final push, he broke free. He darted out the aircraft door and into the tunnel.

"I did it! I did it!" he gasped, his heart racing with excitement.

He had escaped from Annie, made it out of the plane and finally arrived in Boston.

"I'm home!" Ty sang joyously, his voice filled with relief and triumph.

40

What happened next was horrifying. Ty watched as Annie and the flight attendant grappled. Annie struggled to free herself from her own tangled web, while the flight attendant tried to shake off the sticky threads clinging to her fingers.

With a sudden, wild wave of her hand, the flight attendant flung Annie onto the floor.

Ty looked down and watched as Annie panicked, running in frantic circles.

He counted aloud, "One, two, three, four, five, six, seven," and was shocked to realize she only had seven legs—Annie had lost a leg during the struggle.

"She's not going to make it," Ty said softly, feeling an unexpected pang of compassion.

He watched as the door began to close, cutting off her escape route.

"Ugh! Why do I care after what she put me through?" he said, torn between leaving her behind and his instinct to help.

Ty flew back onto the plane, determined to save Annie. He fluttered in front of the flight attendant's face, creating just enough of a distraction.

This gave her the chance she needed to hobble out through the plane door. Ty quickly followed, making his final escape just as the heavy door slammed shut behind them.

He looked down at Annie, who was limping swiftly down the tunnel. Cautiously, he flew past her.

Annie glanced up with angry eyes and hissed, "Until we meet again, Ty Fly."

A knot tightened in Ty's stomach, but he shook it off. He couldn't worry about Annie now. The flyball game was waiting, and he was going to be right on time.

Ty Fly	Annie Spider	Mosquito
Co-Pilot Charles	Captain Bessie Coleman	Trans Passenger
Young Hugo	Flight Attendant #1	Flight Attendant #2

A very special thanks to the following:

Sarah, Nina & Nate Macri, Sarah Mochak, Hashy, Mobius Strip, Kerri Brown, Anna Sandbank, Stephen King, the Komenda Family, Sue Komenda: Editor, MET, Debbie Piltch, NFT-Murder.xyz, Mary Rafter, Lisa Marzilli, Samaritans, The Trevor Project, Mix 104.1, Karson Kager, Kennedy Elsey, Producer Dan, Annie Dow, The Good Vibe Tribe, Black Lives Matter, the Commonwealth, Jesse, Tara: BookBaby and Illustrator Hugoshi.

abugtravelsfar.com